Fables & Folktales

The Hare & the Tortoise

by Tyler Gieseke

Dash!
LEVELED READERS
An Imprint of Abdo Zoom • abdobooks.com

Level 1 – Beginning
Short and simple sentences with familiar words or patterns for children who are beginning to understand how letters and sounds go together.

Level 2 – Emerging
Longer words and sentences with more complex language patterns for readers who are practicing common words and letter sounds.

Level 3 – Transitional
More developed language and vocabulary for readers who are becoming more independent.

abdobooks.com

Published by Abdo Zoom, a division of ABDO, PO Box 398166, Minneapolis, Minnesota 55439.

Printed in the United States of America, North Mankato, Minnesota.
102025
012026

Photo Credits: ABDO, Artistly Getty Images, Shutterstock
Production Contributors: Jennie Forsberg, Grace Hansen, Tyler Gieseke
Design Contributors: Candice Keimig, Neil Klinepier, Colleen McLaren

Library of Congress Control Number: 2025936784

Publisher's Cataloging in Publication Data

Names: Gieseke, Tyler, author.
Title: The hare & the tortoise / by Tyler Gieseke
Description: Minneapolis, Minnesota : Abdo Zoom, 2026 | Series: Fables & folktales | Includes online resources and index.
Identifiers: ISBN 9798384940043 (lib. bdg.) | ISBN 9798384940807 (ebook) | ISBN 9798384941187 (read-to-me ebook)
Subjects: LCSH: Tortoises--Juvenile literature. | Aesop's fables--Juvenile literature. | Hares--Juvenile literature. | Running races--Juvenile literature. | Character development--Juvenile literature. | Procrastination--Juvenile literature. | Conduct of life--Juvenile literature. | Fables--Juvenile literature.
Classification: DDC 398.2 [E]--dc23

Table of Contents

Fables & Folktales

Fables and folktales are both kinds of stories. Fables are usually short. They teach a clear **lesson**. They often include talking animals.

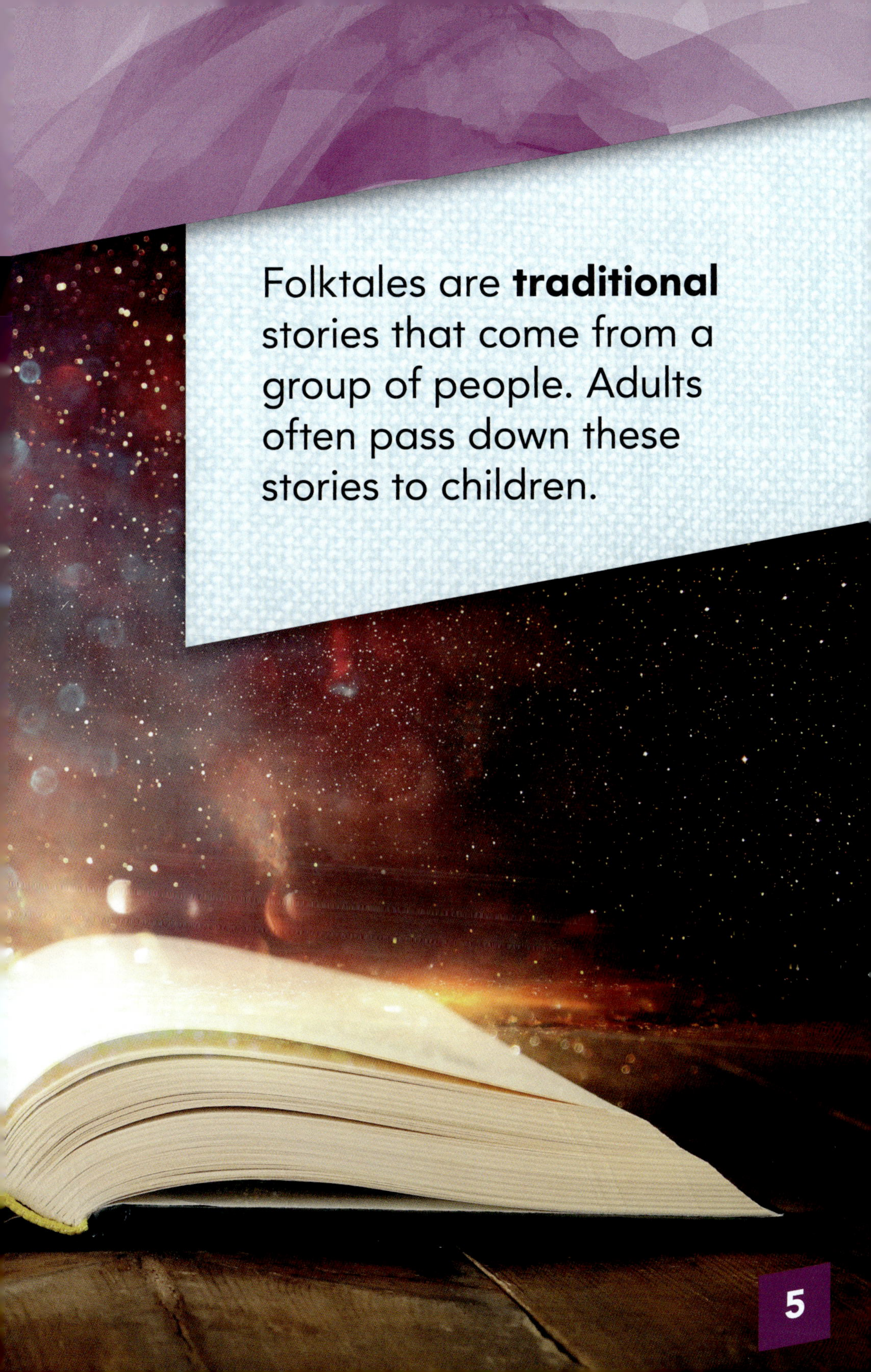

Folktales are **traditional** stories that come from a group of people. Adults often pass down these stories to children.

The Hare and the Tortoise

One well-known fable tells the story of a hare and a tortoise. Once there was a hare who thought he was the fastest animal in the forest. He made fun of the tortoise for being slow. "I'll bet you can't even get to where you want to go," the hare said one day. "But I can get anywhere, quick as can be."

The tortoise was tired of the hare's bragging. "I can move just fine, thank you," he replied. "And you're not as fast as you think. Let's run a race, and I'll show you."

The hare agreed to race the tortoise. He thought he would win easily.

When the race started, the hare quickly took the lead. The tortoise moved forward **steadily**, but he wasn't as fast as the hare. Soon the hare was so far ahead that he could hardly see the tortoise behind him.

The hare wanted the tortoise to feel silly about **challenging** him to a race. So, the hare decided to take a nap! He thought he would still be able to beat the tortoise.

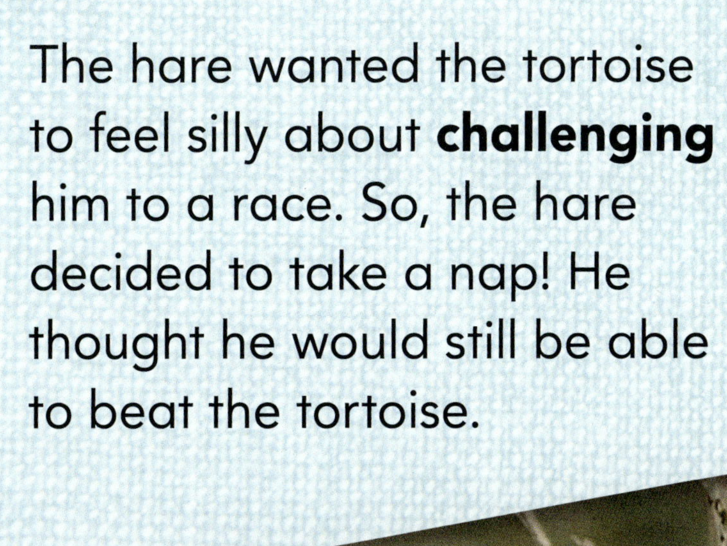

All the while, the tortoise continued to head **gradually** toward the finish line. Eventually he passed the hare, who was fast asleep. The hare awoke to find that the tortoise was almost at the finish line. The hare raced as fast as he could, but it was too late. The tortoise won the race!

Lessons

The main **moral** of this fable is "slow and **steady** wins the race." Even though the hare was clearly faster than the tortoise, this wasn't enough for him to win the race. The tortoise moves slowly but steadily.

He never gives up and never slows down. In contrast, the hare stops partway through. He ends up losing a race that most would expect him to win.

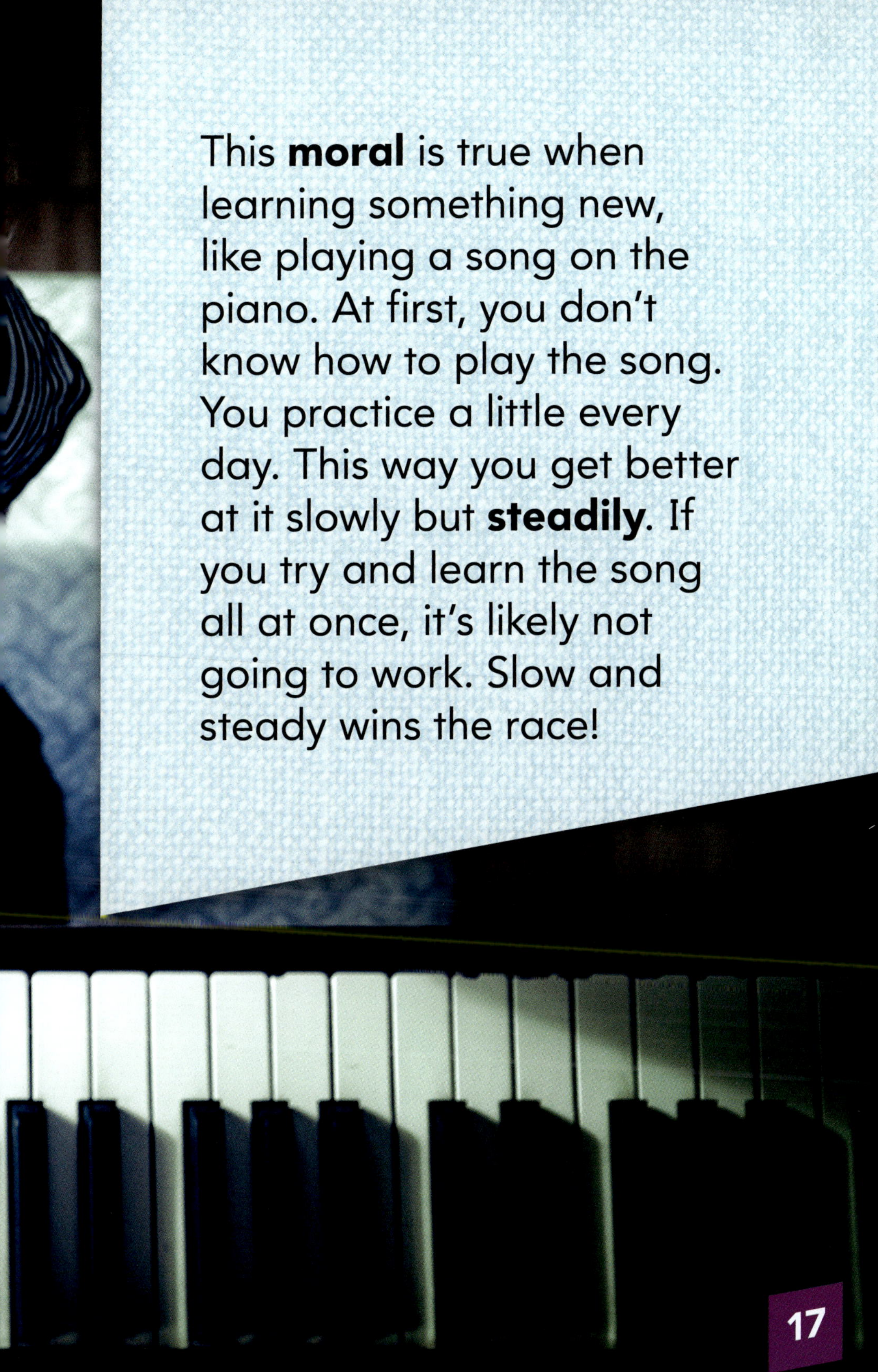

This **moral** is true when learning something new, like playing a song on the piano. At first, you don't know how to play the song. You practice a little every day. This way you get better at it slowly but **steadily**. If you try and learn the song all at once, it's likely not going to work. Slow and steady wins the race!

Another **lesson** from this fable is that too much **confidence** is not a good thing. It makes sense that the hare was excited about his speed. But he was so confident that he thought he could take a nap during a race. This is **arrogance**! It cost him the race.

32

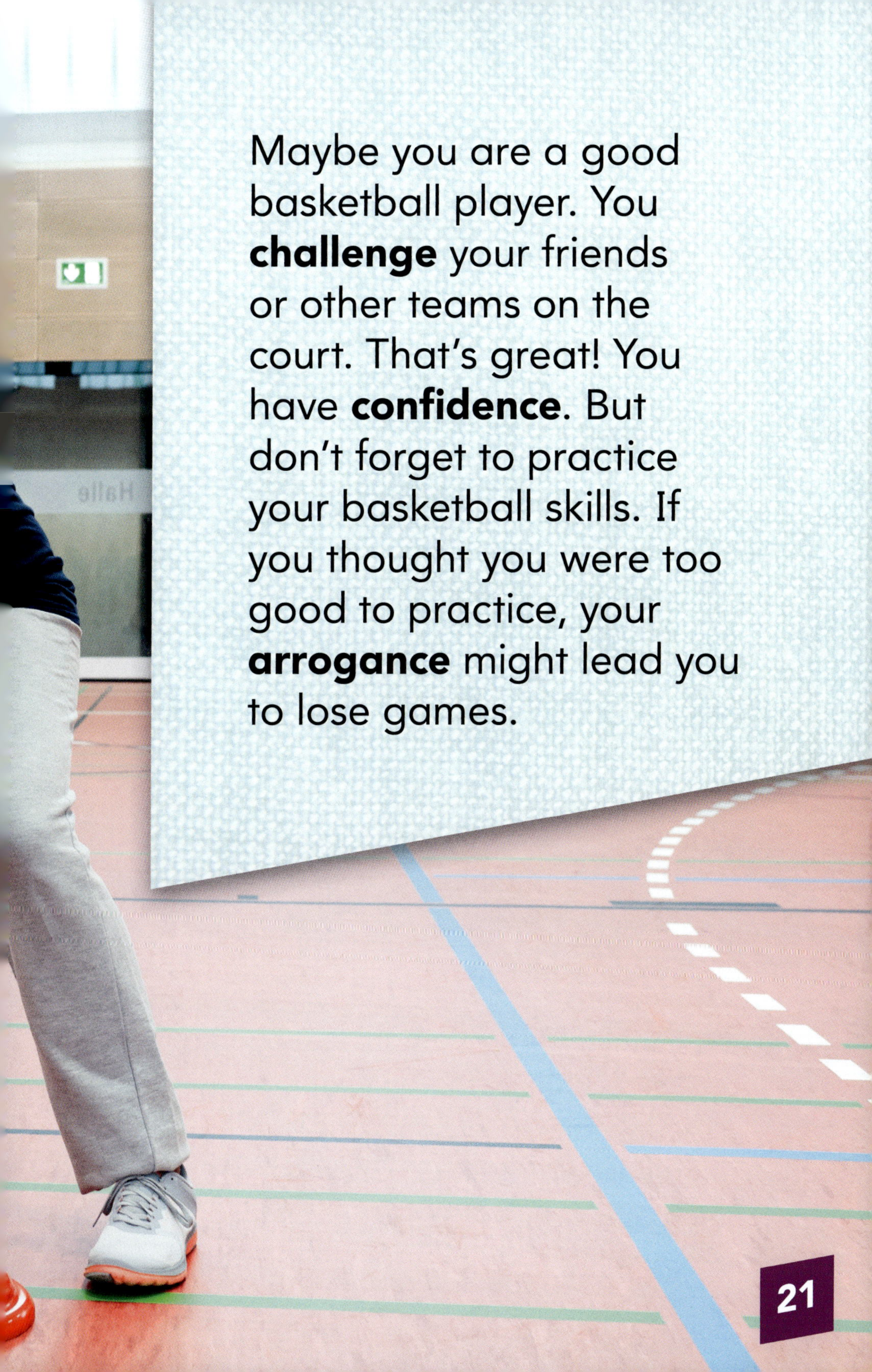

Maybe you are a good basketball player. You **challenge** your friends or other teams on the court. That's great! You have **confidence**. But don't forget to practice your basketball skills. If you thought you were too good to practice, your **arrogance** might lead you to lose games.

More Facts

- *The Hare & the Tortoise* is one of Aesop's fables. These are a famous collection of fables believed to have been written by Aesop.
- Aesop is believed to have been a slave from ancient Greece who later became free. He lived from about 620 to 564 BCE.
- But there are many different versions of Aesop's life and where he came from. Some people even believe Aesop never existed! They think he was made up.
- A tortoise and a hare are carved in marble at the back of the U.S. Supreme Court building in Washington, D.C., to show that justice is slow and **steady**.

Glossary

arrogance – thinking you are much better than other people.

challenge – to dare someone to do something.

confidence – feeling sure about yourself.

gradually – little by little.

lesson – a teaching, or something learned.

moral – a teaching to take away from a story.

steady – not stopping or changing very much; to do something steadily means to not stop.

traditional – describing something done regularly and over time by a group of people.

Index

Online Resources

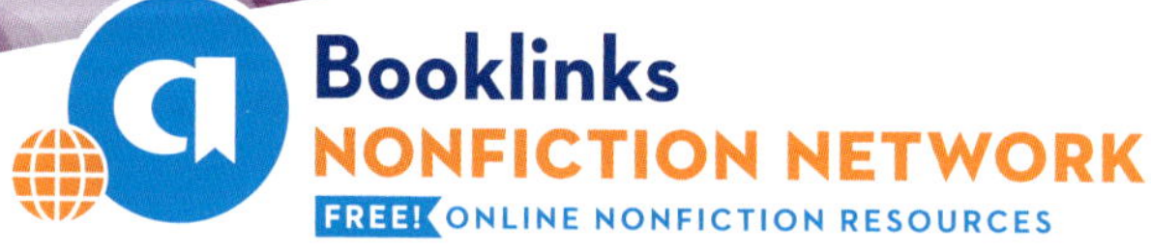

To learn more about *The Hare and the Tortoise*, please visit **abdobooklinks.com** or scan this QR code. These links are routinely monitored and updated to provide the most current information available.